Tacos y Mas

Chef KAREN RAMBO

Photography PAULA JANSEN

Text by CAROL HARALSON

RESORT GIFTS UNLIMITED

TEMPE, ARIZONA

To all the sous chefs in my family,
for so many wonderful hours of cooking together . . . .
Hal, Dana, Stevie, and Beth . . . I love you!

—KAREN RAMBO

The text type was set in Monotype Pastonchi
The display type was set in Bureau Gothic 79
Composed in the United States of America
Design by Trina Stahl
Art Direction and Editing by Carol Haralson
Production Supervision by Todd Atkins
Resort Gifts gratefully acknowledges TasteBuds Gourmet Cooking School,
Sedona, Arizona, for the full use of their kitchen.

Manufactured in Singapore by Tien Wah Press

FIRST IMPRESSION

Library of Congress Catalog Card Number: 98-88190
International Standard Book Number: 189179504X

Distribution rights to titles published by Resort Gifts are held by La Cocina
Cookbook Company, a division of Resort Gifts Unlimited, Incorporated.
Website address: www.resortgifts.com

10 9 8 7 6 5 4 3 2 1

Contents

Y MAS

Introduction

IN MEXICAN COOKING, the traditional taco—whose name means simply "stuffed" or "filled"—is a warm, pliable corn tortilla, tenderly patted into shape and heated on a comal, with a stripe of spicy meat or a few slivers of vegetables adorning it. Enthusiastic diners garnish it themselves with salsa, chiles, onion, cheese, avocado, a squeeze of lime (or many other choices, depending on regional tradition and the cook's resources), then roll or fold it into a tidy package and devour it.

Fresh, simple, and succulent, the taco has understandably become a staple of the Southwestern table. North of the border, however, taco purveyors have tended to standardize their offerings. Drive-through taco chains, while they may make a toothsome fast meal, have made the taco predictable. Deep-fried into a crunchy U-shape, stuffed with seasoned ground beef, and top-dressed with lettuce and tomato, the classic Americanized taco only faintly suggests the many possibilities of the dish.

The great beauty of the taco—besides its blood-warming spice and sustaining combination of grain and meat—is its endless potential for variation. It is as adaptable as the North American sandwich. The tortilla foundation can be thick or thin; it can be made of corn or of white, blue, or whole-wheat flour; it can be fried, dry-toasted, or steamed. Toppings are vegetarian or meat-based, shredded or sliced, grilled, smoked, simmered, or baked. Sauces may be searing or soothing, long-

cooked or quickly whisked, pungent or unguent. Garnishes—
truly the epitome of Mexican-inspired cuisine—are frilly or
plain, many or few, and, even when as simple as a fresh chiffonade of lettuce, add texture, color, and inflections of flavor
characteristic of this delectable, long-evolved dish.

In many ways, the "liberated" taco is utterly appropriate to
contemporary American life. It is fast, fresh, and savory. It
invites the cross-cultural surprises and culinary fusions we have
come to enjoy. And at the same time, it embodies a deep and
soul-satisfying tradition.

Tacos y Mas celebrates the lively taco in two parts. The
Tacos section brings you fresh inspirations on the theme with
14 master recipes. The section called *Y Mas* —"and more" in
Spanish—is a treasury of accompaniments, sauces, garnishes,
marinades, and side dishes to combine in any number of ways
with the taco recipes.

Imagine, experiment, combine and recombine. Fresh Fruit
Salsa is suggested with Jalapeño-Glazed Pork Tenderloin Tacos,
but why not try it with roasted vegetables? Pungent, silky
Cilantro Cumin Crème is fabulous with smoked salmon, but it
would make grilled chicken happy too. The recipe may suggest
a lightly toasted corn tortilla, but why not try a steamed one
made of whole wheat? The taco is just a form, like a song. You
create the words and the melody.

And we promise they will be wonderful.

TORTILLAS

UNDER THE SLASH of coal-charred flank steak, under the
cloud of crisp-fried fish, under the carnival of caramelized
peppers, lies a base as ancient as Latin culture—and older.

Flat-baked, grain-based cakes are probably almost as old as manmade fire.

Traditional tacos were made only with corn tortillas, but with the advent of wheat culture in northern Mexico came flour tortillas, a staple of the American Southwest, and an alternative foundation for the taco.

Corn tortillas are made from a dough called masa. Masa is ground white field corn that has been cooked, soaked with powdered limestone, and hulled. It has an earthy perfume and the texture of stiff cookie dough. You can make your own tortillas using store-bought masa (find it fresh or frozen at your grocers, or purchase from a Mexican restaurant or Hispanic market). Where fresh masa is elusive, you may find masa harina, a dry product sold alongside flour in many markets (Quaker is one reliable brand). Masa harina is dehydrated fresh masa. Reconstitute it by adding water according to package directions.

To make tortillas, pinch off a walnut-sized piece of masa and roll it into a ball. Place it in a tortilla press (made of two hinged metal disks) between pieces of waxed paper and press flat. Or you can press and pat the masa into a tortilla by hand. Place the tortilla in a hot, ungreased skillet and cook about 30 seconds, till the edges begin to brown, then flip and cook briefly till lightly speckled. Turn a second time and cook another 30 seconds or so.

Flour tortillas are made with all-purpose wheat flour. The basic recipe calls for 2 cups flour, 1 teaspoon salt, ½ teaspoon baking powder, ¼ cup lard or shortening, and ½ cup warm water. Mix the dry ingredients together, then cut in the shortening as if for pie crust. Work in the water gradually to make a stiff dough, then knead until the dough is springy. Divide the dough into balls of equal size and allow them to rest, covered, for half an hour. Use a rolling pin to flatten the balls into thin circles about eight inches across. Bake in a hot, ungreased skillet until speckled—a bit less than two minutes per side.

If you don't wish to make your own tortillas, good ready-made ones will work fine for the recipes in this book. Look for them in your local supermarket or in Hispanic markets. Sometimes you can buy excellent house-made ones from restaurants.

PREPARING TORTILLAS FOR TACOS

Steaming tortillas

TO STEAM: Add water to a steamer or a large saucepan with a steamer basket, cover, and bring the water to a mellow boil. Wrap tortillas in a heavy kitchen towel, fold it shut, and lay it in the steamer. Cover with a tight lid and steam one minute. Remove the steamer from heat and allow it to stand 15 minutes before removing the lid.

Toasting a flour tortilla in a dry skillet

TO TOAST WITHOUT OIL: Heat a wide heavy ungreased skillet. Toast tortillas one at a time, turning once, until crisp and freckly. You can also toast tortillas on the bare rack of a toaster-oven or, with caution not to burn, under a broiler.

TO PAN-TOAST WITH OIL: Add ½ teaspoon of butter to the skillet and heat till it foams but is not yet coloring. Add a tortilla to the skillet and toast, turning once. Or pan-toast with olive oil if preferred.

Flat-frying a corn tortilla

FOR CRISPY TACO SHELLS: Add corn oil to a heavy Dutch oven to a depth of one inch. Heat to 380°F. Slide a tortilla into the oil and fry about 15 seconds, or until it begins to float. Fold into a taco shape, using tongs, and turn. Cook a few seconds more, remove from oil, and drain. (Alternatively, you can flat-fry the tortillas.) If tortillas are very fresh, lay them out to dry for 15 minutes before frying to ensure crispness.

Slicing tortillas for frizzles

TO DEEP-FRY WITH A TACO UTENSIL: Place one tortilla in a long-handled metal taco mold. This utensil holds the tortilla in a U shape while frying. Add corn oil to a tall heavy saucepan or fryer to the depth of one tortilla's diameter. Heat to 380°F. Submerge the tortilla in the utensil under oil till crisp and lightly browned. Remove and drain.

Frying tortilla frizzles

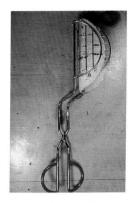

Taco mold available from kitchen supply stores

MAKING TRIANGLE CHIPS OR TORTILLA FRIZZLES: Add two to three inches of corn oil to a heavy skillet and heat to 380°F. Cut corn or flour tortillas into triangles or thin strips. Toss a handful into the oil. Watch closely; the moment they start to color, be prepared to scoop them out of the oil using wide tongs. They will continue to grow browner and crisper for a few minutes after you remove them from the hot oil. Drain on paper towels. Salt while warm, if desired.

CHILES

WHAT OTHER VEGETABLE do you know that has a fan club and a magazine devoted to it? And, though it is purveyed with greenstuff, is technically a fruit or a berry? And is used as a vegetable, a condiment, a spice—and even a medicine. The chile (whose name comes from the ancient Nahuatl word *chilli*), is indeed strange fruit.

A book could be written about the miraculous chile—and many have. Here we will be brief. Experiment with chiles in your area. As the American palate grows steelier, they increase in abundance. But take the labels with a grain of salt. Less common chiles are often misnamed.

In the fresh bins, look for square-shouldered, dark green, moderately hot poblanos; green or ripe-red bullet-shaped jalapeños; dark-red hot serranos the width of your little finger;

Toasting chiles

hottest-of-all small lantern-shaped habaneros; and fairly mild long green New Mexico chiles, sometimes called Anaheims. When dried, these turn red, as do most green chiles. They are the dried chile you see in long garlands called *ristras*. They are available throughout the Southwest in supermarkets, often from a rack or display with dried Mexican oregano and packets of ground chile.

Where dried chiles are available, you may also find anchos (dried poblanos), mulatos (dark, chocolatey chiles much like dried poblanos but deeper in taste), and the indispensible chipotle (a smoke-dried jalapeño).

Choose your ground chile, or chile powder, with the care you would lavish on an important gift. Buy it pure and fresh. Keep it well protected in the freezer for longest life. Be aware that common commercial "chile powders" are usually mixed with various powdered spices such as cumin, which may be of uncertain grade. If good ground chile is not available, you may wish to toast and grind your own. It is quickly done.

Smaller chiles are often—but not always—hotter than large ones. The deep heat is in the seeds and membranes, so you can control it to an extent by discarding these.

GARNISHES AND ACCOMPANIMENTS

IN TRADITIONAL AMERICAN cooking, garnish once meant a sprig of parsley, like a boutinniére, which migrated around the plate as the diner dodged it with his fork until dinner was finished.

This is *not* what garnish means to a taco.

Taco garnishes are integral to the completed dish. Diners may often garnish their own tacos, arriving at the exact combination of zing, crunch, and comfort they prefer at the moment.

Have fun with garnishes—the sky's the limit. Try crumbles of Mexican queso fresco (fresh cheese), queso añejo (aged cheese), or queso seco (dried cheese); bright salty feta, grated mellow jack, or other cheeses; pickled vegetables or chiles; roasted chile strips (marinated in oil and vinegar for moistness and punch); scribbles of lettuce; radishes; toasted nuts or seeds; sprouts; avocado fans or guacamole; minced red onion; Pico de Gallo or other salsas; olives; chopped tomato.

BUILDING A TACO is like writing a poem, or maybe a rock song. Respecting the basic architecture, use the materials at hand, or those you most favor. Combine them with feeling. This is food to have fun with, and to share.

Tacos

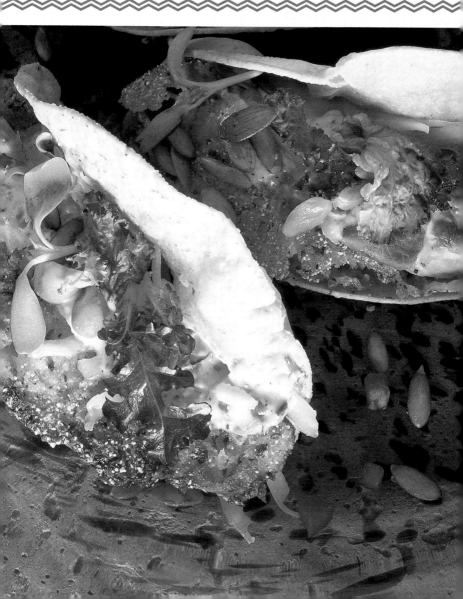

Tacos del Campo

"DEL CAMPO" MEANS *"country-style" and these little tacos are indeed the "chicken-fried steak" of Mexico. They are also astonishingly good.*

SERVES 6

36 corn tortillas, 4½ inches in diameter

2 cups finely grated cabbage

1½ pounds flank or skirt steak

3 tablespoons finely minced garlic

½ cup coarsely chopped cilantro

1 teaspoon cumin seeds, toasted and ground

1 teaspoon coriander seeds, toasted and ground

1 teaspoon dried Mexican oregano

3 tablespoons fresh lime juice

1 teaspoon sugar

1 teaspoon kosher salt

1 teaspoon freshly cracked black pepper

4 tablespoons olive oil

GARNISH

2 limes, quartered

Chile-Pickled Carrots (page 50) for garnish

sliced fresh cucumbers for garnish

chopped cilantro for garnish

salsa, if desired

Guacamole, if desired

In a medium bowl, combine all ingredients except flank steak to make a marinade. Settle the steak in the bowl of marinade and allow to marinate at room temperature at least 30 minutes but not longer than two hours.

TO GRILL

Prepare grill and oil racks. Drain steak and sear on grill over medium-high heat for five to six minutes each side for medium rare.

OVEN METHOD

Preheat oven to 400°F. Place beef in a shallow heavy cooking pan and roast five to six minutes per side. Steak is done when it registers 140°F on a meat thermometer. Watch closely so as not to overcook.

Allow beef to rest 10 minutes. Slice against the grain into ½-inch slices and then into julienne strips.

Toss the cabbage with the beef.

To serve, lay two tortillas atop one another and top with a large spoonful of beef-cabbage mixture. Squeeze lime juice over and sprinkle with chopped cilantro.

Offer tacos with lime wedges, Chile-Pickled Carrots, and fresh sliced cucumbers.

Crispy Sole Tacos with Toasted Pumpkin Seeds

Crispy Sole Tacos combine the hot crunch and delicate flavor of pan-seared fish fillets with a traditional corn tortilla. Caper Sauce adds the zing usually associated with chile-fired salsa, and offers a suave, creamy texture. Sole is a good choice, but red snapper, orange roughy, and other white-fleshed fish work well, as long as the fillets are thin enough to cook quickly (about ¼ inch in thickness) and firm enough to hold together in the skillet. (See page 15.)

SERVES 4

1 teaspoon peanut or vegetable oil

½ cup hulled, raw, unsalted pumpkin seeds

4 crispy taco shells made with corn tortillas (page 10)

4 fillets of sole

½ cup bread crumbs made from toasted French bread

½ cup stone-ground cornmeal

½ teaspoon cayenne chile powder

¼ teaspoon freshly ground black pepper

½ teaspoon kosher salt

1 tablespoon finely chopped fresh parsley

1 tablespoon finely chopped fresh dill

¾ cup milk

½ cup all-purpose flour

½ cup corn or peanut oil

2 tablespoons olive oil
2 tablespoons red wine vinegar
1 to 2 cups mixed baby lettuces
Caper Sauce (page 57)

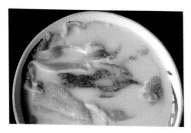

Dip fish fillet into milk

Coat fish fillet with flour

Turn fish fillet in bread crumbs

Heat the oil in a heavy skillet. Add seeds and toast till crunchy, about five minutes, stirring constantly. Remove to paper towels, salt if desired, and set aside.

In a shallow bowl, combine the bread crumbs, cornmeal, cayenne, black pepper, salt, parsley, and dill. In a second bowl pour the milk. Put the flour in a third bowl.

Dip the fish fillets one at a time first into milk, then into flour, then into milk a second time, then into the bread crumb mixture, coating generously. Refrigerate 15 minutes to encourage coatings to adhere.

Heat the oil over medium-high heat in a large, heavy skillet (cast iron is ideal). When the oil is hot enough to dimple gently but not smoking, test by flicking a pinch of flour into the skillet. The flour should foam quickly but not burn. Slide the fillets into the oil gently, taking care not to overcrowd (which will lower the oil temperature too much). Fillets should not touch.

Sauté until brown and crispy, turning once. This will take about three minutes per side. Remove fish to a wire rack in order to keep their undersides crisp, and if necessary keep warm in a 200°F oven.

Whisk the oil and vinegar together in a large bowl to make a vinaigrette and toss the lettuce in it just to moisten.

Gently slide a crispy fillet into each folded tortilla and spoon a dollop of Caper Sauce over. Add lettuce and sprinkle with toasted pumpkin seeds.

Kosher salt marries southwestern flavors

Roasted Vegetable Envelopes

CARAMEL-CHARRED VEGETABLES *are great encased in tortillas. Pair them with Creamy Tortilla Soup (page 55) for a tasty vegetarian meal.*

SERVES 6 AS A SIDE DISH

6 ten-inch flour or whole-wheat tortillas, warmed or
   steamed
1 each red, green, and yellow bell peppers, stemmed,
   seeded, and halved
1 fresh poblano chile, stemmed, seeded, and halved
1 red onion, peeled and halved
10 large mushrooms, cleaned with a damp paper towel
¾ cup Honey-Citrus Marinade (page 58) or garlic-infused
   olive oil, salt, pepper, and a dash of cayenne powder

Put the vegetables in a large glass or ceramic bowl and pour marinade over. Set aside at room temperature one hour.

Prepare the grill and oil racks. Drain vegetables and grill at medium-high heat, turning occasionally, until they are tender-crisp and somewhat blackened. Alternatively, roast them under the broiler at high heat.

Allow vegetables to cool to touch and cut into thick strips. Serve in warm tortillas with favorite accompaniments.

Grilled Skirt Steak Fajitas

THE FOLD∕IT∕YOURSELF *fajita operates on the same principle as simple country tacos dispensed from closet-sized taquerias throughout urban Mexico, except that in the States, fajitas are usually made with flour tortillas and their fillings are presented with sumptuous flourish. These make for a great Cinco de Mayo party.*

SERVES 6

6 ten∕inch flour tortillas
2 to 3 pounds skirt or flank steak
3 tablespoons soy sauce
zest of one lime, minced
zest of one orange, minced
½ cup fresh orange juice
4 tablespoons fresh lime juice
3 tablespoons finely minced fresh garlic
1½ tablespoons balsamic vinegar
1½ tablespoons sugar
1 tablespoon dried rosemary, crumbled
¼ cup extra∕virgin olive oil
1 teaspoon cumin seeds, toasted and ground
1 teaspoon kosher salt
½ teaspoon freshly cracked black pepper

Combine all ingredients except steak and tortillas in a large bowl and whisk lightly to make marinade. Place the steak in a plastic sealable bag and pour the marinade over. Seal and set aside at room temperature one hour.

Prepare the grill and oil racks. Drain steak and grill over medium-high heat six minutes per side for rare; eight for medium doneness. Remove from grill and allow to rest five minutes (so that meat reabsorbs its juices and loses less essence in slicing).

ALTERNATIVE OVEN METHOD

Preheat oven to 400°F. Place beef in a heavy, shallow cooking pan. Cook beef five to six minutes per side, until meat thermometer reaches 140°F for rare or 150°F for medium-rare. Remove from oven and allow to sit for 10 minutes before slicing.

Slice meat thinly and serve with warm flour tortillas and accompaniments such as Guacamole (page 65), shredded lettuce, Pico de Gallo (page 72), Roasted Chiles (page 74), or other favorite garnishes. Invite diners to assemble their own tacos.

For a great buffet party, serve the fajitas alongside Citrus-Marinated Grilled Chicken Tacos (page 29) and the makings for Roasted Vegetable Envelopes (page 23).

Tacos with New Mexican Chile Con Carne

THE BASIC TACO, *with a crunchy shell encasing hot, chile-fragrant ground beef. Make the Chile Con Carne up to two days ahead if desired (it just gets better), or serve it first by the steaming bowlful and a day later in tacos.*

SERVES 8

16 crispy taco shells made with corn tortillas (page 10)
New Mexican Chile Con Carne (page 52), prepared
    without hominy
2 cups coarsely grated cheddar-jack cheese, or 1 cup
    sharp cheddar and 1 cup Monterrey jack, mixed
1½ cups diced tomato
2 cups shredded lettuce

If taco shells are not warm, heat them in the oven on a baking sheet at 350°F approximately 10 minutes. Fill each shell with hot New Mexican Chile Con Carne and top with ¼ cup cheese and ¼ cup lettuce. Garnish with diced tomato and serve warm.

Pass the Guacamole (page 65) and Pico de Gallo (page 72).

Citrus-Marinated
Grilled Chicken Tacos

CITRUS-SCENTED MARINADE *suffuses white meat with flavor and gives it a tender texture. Marinate for only an hour, not more. Otherwise the chicken can become mealy.*

SERVES 6

6 ten-inch flour tortillas
4 chicken breasts, skinned and boned
2 cups Honey-Citrus Marinade (page 58)
Guacamole (page 65) or Fresh Fruit Salsa (page 62)
as an accompaniment
shredded lettuce for garnish

Put chicken in a glass dish or sealable plastic bag and pour marinade over. Allow to stand at room temperature for an hour.

Prepare the grill and oil racks. Remove the chicken from the marinade and drain, reserving marinade. Pour marinade into a small saucepan and bring to a boil. Remove from heat and set aside.

Grill chicken on medium-high heat approximately five minutes each side. Baste generously with marinade while grilling. When chicken is well browned, remove from grill and allow to rest five minutes before cutting into strips.

Preparing to make a chiffonade

Rolling the leaves

Slicing the leaves

Preheat oven to 400°F. Line a heavy baking sheet with foil and arrange chicken in it. Cook six minutes per side until chicken is golden. Do not overcook; chicken is done when juices run clear.

Lightly toast tortillas one at a time in a heavy dry skillet. Remove from skillet while still pliable and fill with chicken strips. Fold over taco style and return to skillet. Press shut and toast lightly on both sides.

Garnish and serve.

Grilled Pesto Shrimp Tacos

GRILLED PESTO SHRIMP TACOS *are an inviting first course. Single shrimp supported by small crisp tortilla wedges make a great pick-up hors d'oeuvre.*

SERVES 4 AS AN APPETIZER

4 corn tortillas, fried flat and crisp in a lightly oiled skillet
1¼ cups Cilantro Pesto (page 60)
1 pound medium-sized raw shrimp, washed, deveined,
    and dried with paper towels
2 cups thinly sliced cabbage
½ cup mayonnaise
purple cabbage or kale for garnish, if desired

Soak four long wooden skewers in water to prevent burn-ing on the grill.

Turn shrimp in Cilantro Pesto to coat thickly. This is easi-est to do with your bare hands. Allow to marinate at room temperature 30 minutes. Remove skewers from soaking water and thread shrimp on them. Prepare the grill and oil racks. Heat grill to medium-high. Grill shrimp approximately three minutes per side, remove from grill, and set aside.

ALTERNATIVE OVEN METHOD

Preheat broiler. Line a heavy baking sheet with foil and arrange the shrimp on it. Broil until pink and crispy, about three to four minutes per side. Do not overcook or shrimp will be tough. Each broiler is different, so watch the shrimp closely.

Whisk the mayonnaise with ¼ cup Cilantro Pesto in a large bowl. Add cabbage and toss.

To assemble, dollop a spoonful of cabbage onto a crisp tortilla and top with shrimp, either on or off the skewer. Garnish with a sprinkling of minced purple cabbage or kale, if desired.

Jalapeño-Glazed
Pork Tenderloin Tacos

TENDERLOIN GRILLED OR *roasted in a spicy-sweet crust of spices, herbs, and chile retains its delicacy and moistness while acquiring a superb flavor.*

SERVES 6

12 eight-inch corn tortillas
2 pork tenderloins, one pound each
Southwest Seasoning for Pork and Chicken (page 76)
Smoky Jalapeño Glaze (page 61)
small amount of oil or butter for crisping tortillas
    (if desired)
Fresh Fruit Salsa (page 62)
cilantro for garnish
pan-toasted piñon nuts for garnish

Rub tenderloins thoroughly with Southwest Seasoning for Pork and Chicken and allow to sit at room temperature one hour.

Prepare the grill to medium-high heat. Grill the tender-loins, turning every five minutes and basting with the Smoky Jalapeño Glaze. Cook till meat registers 150°F on a meat thermometer.

ALTERNATIVE OVEN METHOD

Preheat the oven to 400°F. Place tenderloins in a pan fitted with a dripping rack and roast 15 to 20 minutes. Baste with glaze, turn, and roast the other side 15 to 20 minutes. Baste again. Test with a meat thermometer for doneness: 140°F for rare, 150°F for medium-rare. If meat is not quite done, continue to roast, turning every five minutes and basting after every turn.

Remove meat and allow to sit five minutes. Set aside.

Prepare the tortillas. Steam them, if you want a soft, pliant taco, or crisp them on both sides in a heavy hot skillet, dry or coated with a ½ teaspoon oil or butter for each taco.

Slice tenderloins into ¼-inch medallions and fan across tortillas. Add a dollop of Fresh Fruit Salsa.

Garnish with fresh cilantro and toasted piñon nuts, if desired.

Spicy Shredded Pork Tacos

THE COOKING BROTH *from the pork is full of flavor and delicious as the base for a "day-after" soup.*

SERVES 6

12 eight-inch corn tortillas, steamed
1 three- to four-pound pork loin with bone
3 small dried hot red chiles, stemmed and seeded
6 garlic cloves, peeled
2 medium-sized white onions, chopped
4 whole bay leaves
6 cups water
3 cups chicken stock or canned chicken broth
2 teaspoons cumin seeds, toasted and crushed
2 tablespoons dried Mexican oregano leaves
2 teaspoons kosher salt
1 teaspoon freshly cracked black pepper
optional garnishes: crumbled queso fresco, diced
     tomatoes, chopped roasted chiles

Put all the ingredients except the tortillas into a large pot and bring to a gentle boil. Simmer, covered, until the pork is very tender, approximately two to three hours. Allow pork to cool in its broth. Shred pork and remove and fat and bone.

Fill steamed tortillas with shredded pork. Pass the salsa or Pico de Gallo (page 72) and Guacamole (page 65) and your choice of garnishes.

Smoked Salmon Tacos with Cilantro Cumin Crème

SMOKED SALMON TACOS *make an amazingly fast but mouth-watering hors d'oeuvre. A batch of Cilanto Cumin Crème will be more than you need for this recipe; refrigerate the rest for up to several days and enjoy it on sandwiches or with roast chicken. A dollop adds velvet and fire to a bowl of soup.*

SERVES 4 AS AN APPETIZER

4 eight-inch flour tortillas
4 thin slices of smoked salmon
1 cup Cilantro Cumin Crème (page 64)
fresh dill for garnish

Place a large dry heavy skillet over medium-high heat. Place the tortillas in it one at a time, turning once, to crisp. Spread Cumin Cilantro Crème on each tortilla and top with salmon. Slice in quarters, garnish with dill, and serve.

Oven-Dried Tomato, Basil, and Pine Nut Tacos

OVEN-DRIED TOMATOES *are to sliced store-bought tomatoes as a live concert is to the telephone music you hear while on hold. Even pallid winter tomatoes get such a concentrated kick from oven-drying that you will find dozens of uses for them (think salads, quesadillas, scrambled eggs, sandwiches). They keep well in a tightly sealed glass jar.*

SERVES 8

8 eight-inch flour tortillas
4 ripe tomatoes, sliced thinly and evenly
1½ cups coarsely grated Monterrey jack cheese
½ cup pine nuts, toasted in a dry skillet till lightly brown
1 cup fresh basil leaves
olive oil
kosher salt
freshly cracked black pepper

Preheat the oven to 250°F. Line a heavy baking sheet with parchment and dot it with the tomato slices. Bake until the slices brown lightly, about 45 minutes to an hour. Check occasionally as outer slices and thinner ones brown fastest. Turn the pan once or twice for even cooking and remove slices as they appear done, if necessary. If they brown too much, their

Slice the tomatoes

Season the slices

flavor has a hint of bitterness. When tomatoes are done, remove from the oven and increase oven temperature to 400°F.

Heat a large sauté pan over medium-high heat. Sear each tortilla in the pan, turning once, until crisp and freckly.

Line the baking sheet with fresh parchment and arrange the tortillas on it. Sprinkle with cheese and top with oven-dried tomato slices. Scatter with pine nuts. Slide into the hot oven and bake just until cheese is melted. Garnish with basil. Serve immediately.

Remove from oven when brown

Ground Sirloin Tacos
with Black Olive Salsa

Unlike other tacos in this book, these little crowd-pleasers are stuffed with uncooked filling and then pan-fried—so that tortilla and filling cook together. Everything but the final cooking can be done well ahead of time, so they are kind to the cook who wants to come to the party.

SERVES 6 TO 8

25 to 30 fresh corn tortillas, 4½ inches in diameter
1 pound extra-lean ground sirloin
kosher salt
freshly cracked black pepper
corn oil to fill skillet or Dutch oven to depth of ¾ inch

GARNISH

3 cups grated cheddar-jack cheese
3 cups shredded lettuce
½ cup Heinz red wine vinegar
Black Olive Salsa (page 71)
Guacamole (page 65)
chopped roasted green chiles for garnish
bottled hot pepper sauce

Spread three tablespoons of ground sirloin on half of each tortilla. Sprinkle with salt and pepper. This can be done several hours ahead of cooking; stack, cover with plastic wrap, and refrigerate.

If you are preparing ahead of time, wash, dry, and shred the lettuce (quickest with the chiffonade technique) and store it in a sealable plastic bag in the refrigerator. Store grated cheese the same way.

Add oil to a large heavy skillet and heat to 350°F. Slip one open-faced taco at a time into the oil. When it bobs toward the top, fold it and press it shut with a pair of tongs, continue to cook until it is crisp and the meat is done. Depending on the breadth of your skillet, you may be able to cook two or three tacos at a time. Keep finished tacos warm in a 200°F oven.

When tacos are ready to serve, toss the lettuce in the red wine vinegar.

To serve, set forth hot tacos, cheese, Black Olive Salsa, and lettuce. Invite diners to dress up their own tacos.

Y Mas Cocktail Tacos

Mix the Margueritas, serve up the fruit-steeped Sangría, put an opener by the iced Mexican beer—and make it a fiesta. One-bite, big-night cocktail tacos take advantage of almost every recipe in this book—so that any treasured extras from a more substantial dish can be combined in dozens of ways. Lay out all your treasures and play.

> corn or flour tortillas cut with a biscuit cutter into
>   two-inch rounds
> bite-size morsels of grilled meat, fish, and/or chicken
> dabs of sauce: Cilantro Cumin Crème, Cilantro Pesto,
>   Pico de Gallo, Black Olive Salsa
> roasted mushrooms, peppers, onions
> various cheeses, shredded, crumbled, or grated
> oven-dried tomatoes
> sprigs of dill, basil, other fresh herbs
> toasted pumpkin seeds and piñon nuts

Preheat the oven to 400°F. Line a heavy baking sheet with parchment. Arrange tortilla rounds on the parchment.

Top the rounds with all the possible combinations. Work quickly, choosing combinations that look tasty. Cheese is a good "cement" for elements that want to stray. Top with fresh sprigs or add them when the tacos are baked.

Bake approximately five minutes, or until cheese melts and tacos are beginning to color around the edges.

Arizona Cowboy
Potato Tacos

THE QUESADILLA-STYLE *method of pan-toasting filled tacos called for here is a great technique to remember. It works with any number of spontaneously invented fillings, even a combination as simple as cheese and a sprig of fresh basil, with great results.*

SERVES 4 TO 6 AS A SIDE DISH

6 eight-inch flour tortillas
1 fresh ear of corn
2 tablespoons butter
4 tablespoons corn oil
4 green onions, chopped with part of green tops
½ cup each finely diced red, green, and yellow stemmed
    and seeded bell peppers
2 tablespoons seeded and finely diced jalapeño chile
4 cups Yukon Gold potatoes (no need to peel),
    diced evenly into ¼-inch-square cubes
2 cloves garlic, minced
1 tablespoon Chile Blend for Tacos y Mas (page 77)
    or red chile powder
1 teaspoon kosher salt
½ teaspoon freshly cracked black pepper
1½ cups grated pepper-jack cheese

Roast the ear of corn over an open gas flame, on the grill, or in the broiler, and set aside. When cool enough to handle, slice kernels from the cob.

Heat butter and oil in a large heavy skillet. Add green onions, peppers, and jalapeño. Sauté until soft. Add diced potatoes, garlic, Chile Blend or red chile powder, salt, and pepper and stir. Cover for three minutes. Uncover and stir potatoes so that they brown evenly. Cover again and cook three minutes more. Stir in corn kernels. Cook, uncovered, until potatoes are brown and tender. Remove from heat and set aside.

Spoon potato mixture onto one side of each tortilla and top with cheese. Fold each tortilla in half to enclose filling.

In a large clean sauté pan over medium heat, heat ½ teaspoon of butter until it sizzles and just begins to color (do not let it brown). Slide a taco into the pan and toast. Flip and toast on the other side, making sure the cheese melts. Repeat for remaining tacos. Slice tacos into halves and serve hot.

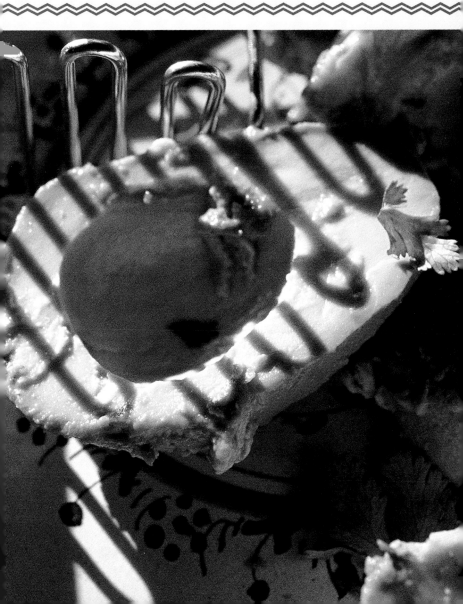

y Mas

Chile-Pickled Carrots

TAQUERIAS OFTEN SERVE *pickled carrots with country-style tacos. Crunchy, bright "carrot pickles" keep well; the flavors blend and mellow over time.*

MAKES 1 QUART

3 large sweet carrots

¼ cup thinly sliced white onion

5 garlic cloves, smashed, peeled, and roughly chopped

1 teaspoon dried Mexican oregano leaves

½ teaspoon cumin seed

5 whole peppercorns

1 sixteen-ounce jar whole pickled jalapeño peppers, with pickling juice

½ teaspoon sugar

2 tablespoons kosher salt

1 cup cider vinegar

1 tablespoon canola oil

Peel carrots and slice them thinly lengthwise.

Place carrots in a large bowl with onion, garlic, oregano, cumin, peppercorns, and jalapeños.

Combine sugar, salt, vinegar, and oil in a medium saucepan and heat until sugar and salt have dissolved. Pour over carrot mixture and stir well.

Store pickled carrots, tightly sealed, in the refrigerator. They will last several weeks.

New Mexican Chile Con Carne

IN SPANISH, THIS *classic dish is Chile Con Carne, or "chile with meat," not Carne Con Chile, "meat with chile." The emphasis makes it clear how important good ground chile is to the final result. If you don't have access to fresh, intense ground chile, you can make your own by pan-toasting and grinding stemmed and seeded anchos (dried poblanos), New Mexican red chiles, or other hot chiles. Chile Con Carne makes a great do-ahead meal as it improves if refrigerated overnight.*

SERVES 8

2 pounds lean ground beef

1 large yellow onion, peeled and diced

2 large green bell peppers, stemmed, seeded and diced

2 large poblano chiles, stemmed, seeded and diced

2 tablespoons corn oil

6 large garlic cloves, peeled and diced

1 twenty-eight-ounce can tomatoes, with juice

2 tablespoons New Mexican medium-hot red chile powder

2 tablespoons ancho chile powder

1 tablespoon each cumin seed, coriander seed, and dried Mexican oregano leaves toasted together in a dry skillet, cooled, and ground in a coffee grinder or mortar

3 cups beef stock or au jus concentrate diluted with water
½ teaspoon sugar
½ teaspoon kosher salt
½ teaspoon freshly cracked black pepper
1 sixteen-ounce can cooked drained hominy, if desired

GARNISH

cheddar-jack cheese, grated, as an optional topping
tortilla frizzles for garnish, if desired (page 10)

In a large soup pot or Dutch oven over medium-high heat, sauté the onion, peppers, and chiles in the corn oil until soft, about 10 minutes. Add garlic and sauté three minutes.

Add ground beef and sauté until beef is brown and liquid has disappeared. Lower heat to medium and add chile powders and spice mixture. Add tomatoes, sugar, salt, pepper, and beef stock.

Add hominy if desired.

Simmer over low heat, uncovered, one hour or longer, until chile is thick and meat is tender. Adjust seasonings to suit your palate.

Ladle up hot Chile Con Carne and dress with grated cheese and tortilla frizzles.

Creamy Tortilla Soup with Frizzles

SOOTHING AND SURPRISINGLY *light in feeling, Creamy Tortilla Soup is also adaptable. And it's very fast—about 35 minutes start to finish. Add shredded roast chicken or kernels of roasted corn if you wish.*

SERVES 4 TO 6

2 tablespoons olive oil

1 cup finely diced white onion

3 garlic cloves, minced finely

3 large poblano chiles, roasted, seeded, and diced

8 ounces canned Ro⟋Tel pepper tomato mixture
(or 1 cup diced tomatoes and one finely minced whole jalapeño chile)

8 ounces canned cream of mushroom soup, undiluted

8 ounces chicken or vegetable stock

1 cup half and half or whole milk

8 ounces processed cheese or sharp cheddar cheese, cubed

2 tablespoons dried Mexican oregano

½ cup chopped cilantro

1 teaspoon kosher salt

½ teaspoon freshly cracked black pepper

GARNISH

Guacamole (page 65)

tortilla frizzles (page 10)

1 cup grated cheddar cheese

Heat a large Dutch oven and sauté onion in oil till soft and translucent, about 10 minutes. Add garlic and sauté three minutes. Add chiles and sauté four minutes. Add soup and stir till blended.

Add Ro*Tel, half and half, cubed cheese, broth, oregano, cilantro, salt, and pepper. Stir until cheese has melted. Simmer over low heat 20 minutes. Make the frizzles while the soup is simmering.

Top servings with dollops of Guacamole, tortilla frizzles, and sprinklings of grated cheese.

Caper Sauce

MAKE THIS SAUCE, *and all the dishes in this book, with kosher salt rather than standard table salt for the best flavor. Kosher salt has a magical way of marrying flavors.*

This velvety, savory sauce loves fish, especially smoked salmon or trout. It also keeps company with sliced beef and tuna salad.

MAKES 2 CUPS

1 cup best-quality mayonnaise
½ cup sour cream or crème fraîche
1 tablespoon finely grated shallot or sharp white onion
2 tablespoons finely grated dill pickle
3 tablespoons coarsely diced brined capers (do not rinse)
3 tablespoons fresh lemon juice
1 teaspoon chopped fresh dill or ½ teaspoon dried dill
1 teaspoon finely chopped fresh oregano or
   ½ teaspoon dried
1 teaspoon finely chopped fresh thyme or
   ½ teaspoon dried
1 teaspoon chopped fresh chives
½ teaspoon kosher salt
½ teaspoon freshly ground black pepper

Combine all ingredients and stir till smooth. Adjust flavor to your taste with small additional amounts of any ingredient. Refrigerate up to one week in a sealed container. Serve at room temperature.

Honey-Citrus Marinade

THIS HIGHLY PERFUMED *marinade is great with chicken, pork, or vegetables destined for the grill or broiler.*

MAKES APPROXIMATELY 2 CUPS

5 garlic cloves, minced fine
1 tablespoon finely diced orange peel
1 tablespoon finely diced lemon peel
1 tablespoon finely diced lime peel
⅓ cup fresh orange juice
¼ cup fresh lemon juice
3 tablespoons fresh lime juice
⅓ cup honey
⅓ cup virgin olive oil
¼ teaspoon ground cumin
¼ teaspoon ground cinnamon
2 tablespoons fresh basil, sliced thinly
1 teaspoon kosher salt
½ teaspoon freshly cracked black pepper

Combine all ingredients in a large bowl and whisk. Use to marinate chicken or pork.

Cilantro Pesto

IN ITS CONCENTRATED STATE, *this pesto is a good marinade for chicken or seafood. Mixed with a little mayonnaise or vinaigrette, it becomes a salad dressing. Follow the same technique with parsley, fresh dill, arugula, or basil for other interesting results.*

MAKES 1 CUP

2 cups firmly packed cilantro leaves
2 garlic cloves
2 tablespoons toasted pine nuts
¾ cup grated Parmesan cheese
2 tablespoons fresh lime juice
2 teaspoons kosher salt
1 teaspoon freshly cracked black pepper
5 tablespoons olive oil

Place all ingredients except oil in a blender or food processor and whirl to combine. With the motor running, slowly add olive oil until the sauce has thickened. Keeps up to two days, covered and refrigerated.

Smoky Jalapeño Glaze

A DELICIOUS BASTING *glaze for pork, chicken, or lamb.*
Smoky Jalapeño Glaze gets its kick from chipotles in adobo, a
canned condiment and cooking ingredient often used in Mexican
cooking. Look for it in the Hispanic section of your supermarket
or in specialty stores.

MAKES 2 CUPS

½ cup diced white onion
⅓ cup plus 2 tablespoons canola oil
¼ cup canned chipotle chiles in adobo sauce, minced
4 teaspoons minced garlic
½ cup honey
¼ cup fresh orange juice
¼ cup fresh lime juice
4 tablespoons rice wine vinegar
½ cup water
1 teaspoon ground cumin
1 teaspoon dried Mexican oregano
1 teaspoon kosher salt
½ teaspoon freshly cracked black pepper

Sauté onions in two tablespoons oil over medium heat
until brown and caramelized. Add garlic and sauté two to
three minutes. Add all the remaining ingredients and cook
over medium heat until the glaze achieves a syrup-like con-
sistency, about 20 to 30 minutes. Cool before using.

Fresh Fruit Salsa

PEACHES ARE A *terrific choice for a colorful salsa when they are juicy and sweet in season. At other times of year, make salsa with mangoes, pineapple, tangerines, or other favorite fruits as they reach their peak of goodness. Citrus juice helps the fruit retain its color. For the brightest flavor, make Fresh Fruit Salsa close to the time you plan to serve it.*

MAKES 4 CUPS

4 tablespoons fresh lime juice

2 tablespoons brown sugar

1 teaspoon kosher salt

4 large, fresh peaches, peeled, pitted, diced (or equivalent volume of another fresh fruit)

½ cup each diced red and green bell pepper

½ cup diced green onion

¼ cup seeded, stemmed, and diced jalapeño chile

¼ cup minced fresh cilantro

¼ teaspoon freshly cracked black pepper

Combine lime juice, brown sugar, and salt in a small bowl. In a separate non-metallic bowl, combine the remaining ingredients. Pour the lime juice mixture over and toss to blend.

Cilantro Cumin Crème

THIS VELVETY, INTENSE *sauce gives a high-voltage flavor kick to smoked salmon or trout. Try it with roast chicken, on sandwiches, or dolloped on tortilla soup.*

MAKES 1 CUP

1 tablespoon plus ¾ teaspoon cumin seeds
1 tablespoon coriander seeds
1 cup crème fraîche or sour cream
2 tablespoons heavy cream
½ cup coarsely chopped cilantro
2 garlic cloves, finely minced
3 tablespoons fresh lime juice
1 teaspoon kosher salt
½ teaspoon freshly cracked black pepper

Combine the cumin and coriander seeds in a small dry sauté pan over medium heat. Roast the seeds, shaking the pan frequently, until they release their spicy perfume and turn golden, about five minutes. Remove from heat. When cool, place in a mortar, spice mill, or clean coffee grinder and pulverize.

Combine the ground spices with the remaining ingredients. Cover and refrigerate at least 30 minutes or up to one day before serving.

Guacamole

THE DEFINITIVE VERSION *of a beloved classic. Make it with an old-fashioned hand-held potato masher, taking care to leave plenty of little chunks of avocado for texture. Small black Haas avocadoes have the best flavor; the large bright green ones from Florida can be watery. Be sure to have the avocadoes at their peak of ripeness, when the flesh yields gently to pressure at the stem end, but the fruits show no deep bruising from age.*

MAKES 3 CUPS

3 large ripe avocadoes, peeled and pitted
1 medium tomato, seeded and finely diced
⅓ medium white onion, finely diced
1 large fresh jalapeño chile, stemmed, seeded, and minced
5 large garlic cloves, peeled and minced
½ teaspoon kosher salt, or more to taste
¼ teaspoon freshly cracked black pepper
½ cup coarsely chopped fresh cilantro
juice of one lime, or more to taste

Combine all ingredients in a glass or ceramic bowl and mash with a hand-held potato masher or large fork. Take care not to overwork the Guacamole; it should stay chunky for best flavor and texture.

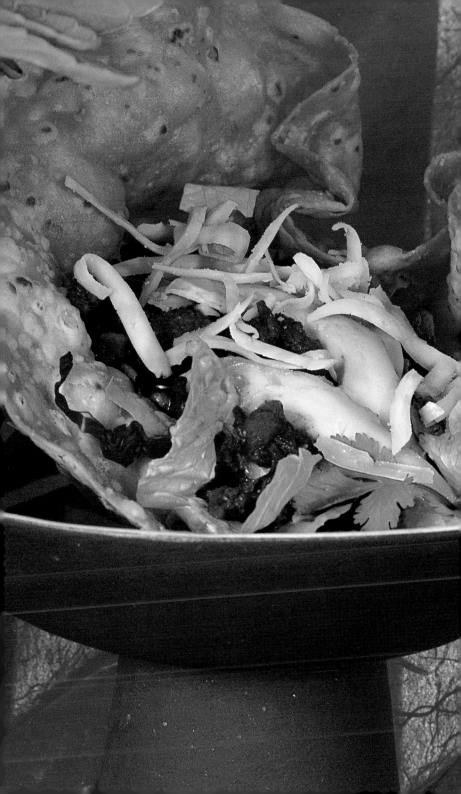

Taco Salad
in Tortilla Bowls

TACO SALAD LOOKS *inviting in crunchy edible bowls like little cornucopias, but the salad is delicious simply served on a bed of toasty tortilla chips. This is a great use for leftover New Mexican Chile Con Carne.*

SERVES 6

6 twelve-inch flour tortillas (burrito style)
corn oil to fill a stock pot to a depth of 6 inches
4 cups chopped mixed Romaine and iceberg lettuce
2 cups ripe tomatoes, diced small
2 cups ripe black olives, coarsely chopped
1½ cups green onions, sliced with part of tops
2 ripe Haas avocadoes, peeled and pitted (sprinkle with
    lime juice to avoid discoloration)
1 cup cilantro, coarsely chopped
New Mexican Chile Con Carne (page 52)
Fire-Roasted Tomato Chipotle Salsa (page 69)
2 cups shredded cheddar-jack cheese

To make tortilla bowls, pour oil into a tall stockpot (eight to nine inches in diameter) till it reaches a depth of about six inches. Heat to 375°F. Place a tortilla in the pot, pushing it under the oil with a large soup ladle placed in its center. Hold it under the oil until it takes the shape of a bowl and becomes crisp and golden, about three minutes. Remove from oil and drain on paper towels. Repeat with remaining tortillas. Be very careful as hot oil may splatter. Tortilla bowls may be made several hours ahead.

To serve, fill each tortilla bowl with layered salad ingredients in the order given, or in the order of your choice. Top with Chile Con Carne and Fire-Roasted Tomato Chipotle Salsa.

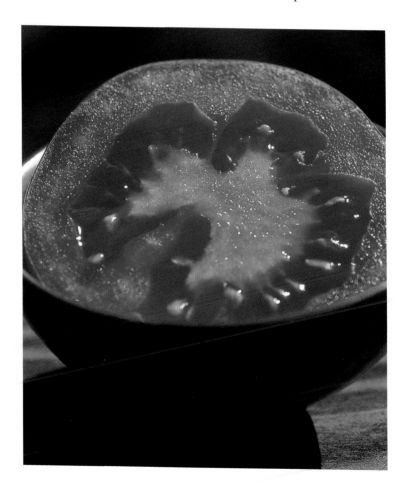

Fire-Roasted
Tomato Chipotle Salsa

LUSCIOUS, DEEPLY-FLAVORED, *cinnabar-colored, this salsa is versatile too. Use it as a dressing for Taco Salad, scoop it up with corn chips as an hors d'oeuvre, or spoon it inside a tortilla with shredded cheese and fresh sprigs of cilantro, fold over, and pan toast for a great breakfast or side dish.*

MAKES 4 TO 5 CUPS

2 whole heads garlic
¼ cup plus 4 tablespoons extra-virgin olive oil
    (divided use)
12 ripe plum tomatoes (about 1 pound)
1 large white onion, peeled and diced small
2 tablespoons Mexican oregano, toasted in a dry skillet
2 teaspoons cumin seeds, toasted and ground to powder
6 to 7 chipotle chiles canned in adobo sauce,
    finely minced
3 tablespoons Heinz red wine vinegar
3 tablespoons freshly squeezed lime juice
1 tablespoon sugar, or to taste
1 tablespoon Chile Blend for Tacos Y Mas (page 77)
1 tablespoon kosher salt, or to taste
1 teaspoon freshly cracked black pepper
¾ cup cilantro, chopped coarsely

Cut ¼ inch off tops of garlic heads, leaving roots whole. Place in a small baking dish and drizzle with 2 tablespoons of the olive oil. Sprinkle with kosher salt and cracked pepper. Cover with foil or a lid and bake at 350°F one hour or until garlic is very soft. Allow garlic to cool, then squeeze the fragrant pulp from each of the cloves in both heads directly into a food processor bowl.

Grill tomatoes on a preheated outdoor grill, or under a hot broiler placed 6 inches from the heat source. Allow to blacken on both sides. Scrape the tomatoes (with blackened residue from the baking sheet, if using the broiler) into the food processor bowl with the garlic. Use a little water if necessary to loosen the browned tomato.

Sauté the onions over medium heat until brown and caramelized. Add the Mexican oregano, cumin, Chile Blend. Stir with onions over medium heat for three minutes. Allow to cool slightly, then scrape into the processor bowl.

Add the chipotles to the processor bowl. Process garlic, tomatoes, onion mixture, and chipotles, pulsing until finely diced. Scrape into large bowl and add vinegar, remaining olive oil, lime juice, sugar, salt, and pepper. Stir in chopped cilantro. Taste and adjust seasonings if necessary.

Chill three hours before serving to allow flavors to marry.

Black Olive Salsa

IT'S SUGGESTED FOR *Ground Sirloin Tacos, but versatile Black Olive Salsa adds depth and savor to other dishes as well (try it with egg dishes or on nachos). Salsa can be made several hours or a day before serving. Cover and refrigerate until ready to use.*

MAKES APPROXIMATELY 2 CUPS

1 cup chopped black olives
3 medium ripe tomatoes, finely diced
1 small white onion, finely diced
1 large jalapeño, stemmed, seeded, and finely diced
1 cup coarsely chopped fresh cilantro
½ teaspoon kosher salt
¼ teaspoon freshly cracked black pepper
2 tablespoons fresh lime juice
1 tablespoon olive oil
dash of Tabasco sauce

Combine all ingredients in a medium-sized serving bowl and toss to blend.

Pico de Gallo

THE INTENSELY FLAVORED, *all-purpose fresh salsa—named for the "beak of the rooster"—Pico de Gallo complements a huge range of Southwestern dishes and is addictive simply scooped onto toasted tortilla triangles and eaten out of hand. It gains depth and balance by maturing overnight in the refrigerator, which allows the Tabasco to mellow and the sugar and vinegar to penetrate the salsa.*

MAKES 4 TO 5 CUPS

4 large ripe tomatoes, finely diced
1 small red onion, finely diced
4 jalapeño chiles, seeded, stemmed, and finely diced
3 tablespoons minced garlic
¾ cup coarsely chopped cilantro
4 tablespoons fresh lime juice
3 tablespoons Heinz red wine vinegar
1 tablespoon sugar
1 tablespoon Tabasco sauce
1 teaspoon kosher salt, or to taste
½ teaspoon freshly cracked black pepper
3 tablespoons olive oil

Combine all ingredients in a non-metallic bowl and stir to blend. Adjust seasonings to taste.

Roasted Chiles

HAVING A BOWLFUL *of plump, succulent strips of roasted sweet pepper or hot chile in the refrigerator is like having a working passport and a credit card with a zero balance. You're prepared for anything. Select peppers and chiles that are firm, shiny, and unblemished. Store them dry (in paper towels if they show moisture) to delay signs of aging.*

> red and green sweet bell peppers or poblanos, anaheims,
>   fresh New Mexico chiles, or other moderately
>   hot chiles
> drizzle of olive oil
> splash of Heinz red wine vinegar or balsamic vinegar

Wash and dry peppers or chiles. Rub them lightly with oil (this causes flames to lick into the crevices and makes peeling easier.) Place them on the burner directly over a live gas flame, or on a heavy round grill made to place over a flame for stove-roasting, available at some kitchen supply stores. Roast, turning as necessary with tongs, until most of the skin has blackened. If you don't have a gas stove, you can do this under the broiler, or on a grill. When chiles are charred, enclose them immediately in a plastic bag and set aside. The steam they release will loosen the skins.

When chiles are cool enough to handle, rub them (still inside the bag) against each other and the plastic bag to loosen and remove the skin. The skin can be bitter, and (especially with green bell peppers) tough; removing it yields a sweet thick strip of chile flesh. It's fine, though, to leave a few small patches of charred skin, which contribute to flavor. Do not rinse chiles or you will rinse away some of the smoky taste.

Split the chiles open and scrape out the seeds and membranes. Remove the stems.

Turn the chiles in a little oil and a teaspoon of red wine vinegar or balsamic vinegar, if desired.

Southwest Seasoning for Pork and Chicken

COOKING WITH THE *freshest, highest quality spices and herbs you can obtain really does make a difference. Toast them to bring out their perfume and deepen their flavors. Ground combinations like this one are robust for months in a tightly sealed jar.*

MAKES ABOUT I CUP

2 teaspoons whole coriander seeds

2 teaspoons cumin seeds

1 teaspoon whole allspice berries

2 teaspoons dried Mexican oregano

1 teaspoon garlic powder

1 teaspoon red chile powder

½ teaspoon freshly cracked black pepper

1 teaspoon kosher salt

1 tablespoon brown sugar

Combine coriander seeds, cumin seed, allspice berries, and oregano in a small dry sauté skillet over medium heat, stirring or shaking the pan as needed until spices are light brown and aromatic, about 10 minutes. Remove from heat. When cool, pour them into a small food processor, clean coffee grinder, or mortar and grind to a powder.

Combine with remaining ingredients.

Chile Blend for Tacos y Mas

STORE CHILE BLEND *in a glass jar with a tight lid away from heat and light. It keeps for months and will enhance a great range of Southwestern cooking, especially long-cooked dishes.*

MAKES ABOUT 2 CUPS

3 tablespoons coriander seeds
3 tablespoons cumin seeds
3 tablespoons dried Mexican
   oregano
¾ cup pure New Mexican red chile
   powder
3 tablespoons ancho chile powder
2 tablespoons paprika
2 tablespoons sugar
2 tablespoons kosher salt

Toasting the spices

Toast coriander and cumin seeds with oregano in a small dry sauté pan, stirring frequently, until they are golden and aromatic, about 10 minutes. Transfer to a spice grinder and pulse till smooth. Combine remaining ingredients, add ground seed mixture, and stir.

Grinding the spices

Frijoles Negros Refritos

BEANS COOK SLOWLY, *but these are worth waiting for. They are so good they are likely to disappear in one meal, but if any are left next day, slather them on a flour tortilla, top with shredded cheddar-pepper cheese, fold shut, and pan-toast quesadilla style (as for Arizona Cowboy Potato Tacos, page 47). You can use pinto beans if preferred.*

SERVES 8 TO 10

1 pound dried black beans
1½ cups chopped white onion
4 large garlic cloves
2 cups chicken stock
½ pound lean smoky bacon, minced
4 jalapeño chiles, finely minced
4 green onions, sliced diagonally with part of green tops
4 tablespoons corn oil
1 teaspoon kosher salt, or to taste
½ teaspoon freshly cracked black pepper
2½ cups coarsely grated cheddar-jack cheese, or
     1 cup sharp cheddar and 1 cup Monterrey jack, mixed

Wash and sort the beans. Place in a stock pot with water to cover by three inches and bring to a boil. Reduce heat and simmer, partially covered, one hour.

Add ¾ cup of the white onions, 2 garlic cloves, and stock

to the beans. Simmer an hour or until beans are tender, adding more water if necessary.

In a large sauté pan, cook the bacon until it is very crisp. Remove the bacon and pour off all but four tablespoons of fat. Sauté remaining onion and garlic, plus jalapeños and green onions, till soft.

Drain the cooked beans, reserving the liquid. Place the beans, bacon, and onion-jalapeño mixture in a food processor and puree. This will have to be done in batches. Combine the pureed batches in a large bowl and stir to blend. You can prepare beans to this stage up to six hours in advance; continue 30 minutes before serving.

Heat the corn oil in a deep, heavy skillet and add the beans. Cook over low heat, stirring constantly, until the beans are thick and some of the liquid has evaporated, about 10 minutes. Stir in 1½ cups of the grated cheese, plus salt and pepper to taste.

Transfer the beans to an oven-proof serving dish and sprinkle with remaining cheese. Bake in a 350°F oven till bubbly, about 20 minutes.

Index